Roam

Also by Laressa Dickey

Bottomland

Laressa Dickey

Roam

Shearsman Books

First published in the United Kingdom in 2016 by
Shearsman Books
50 Westons Hill Drive
Emersons Green
BRISTOL
BS16 7DF

Shearsman Books Ltd Registered Office
30–31 St. James Place, Mangotsfield, Bristol BS16 9JB
(this address not for correspondence)

www.shearsman.com

ISBN 978-1-84861-486-4

Contents

I fly, my dust will be what I am

Hafez (via Borges)

O light open my hand to
impasse

Is it golden, is it
water's wig I wear when I sleep

With desire for misspeaking
angels for ankles

Trolling. Guard [by which I mean
rascal] the field

if I lift up &
roam

A Piece of Information
About His Invisibility

If I had known we were walking here from the bridge
toward home, how we sat, who were we kidding,
I looked at the overturned boats and wept,
tide out, it's just the tide out.

Solo legs draped in purple cloth. Whatever I
touch he straightens. Some say I am homing
but I know I decide. Will my body
be celebratory or just do the washing.

She wasn't stopping along the Atlantic, she was crossing it, by God.
Not worried, she had the hat and aviator glasses,
later I would write away for them from the cereal box address.

I am only the moon on water
I have a kite and storm

He has a tractor he built from plans in *Popular Mechanics*

Reposit: as he says tears when I say I
                    want to buy child shoes. Not dogs
                    nor cats. The domesticated substitutes
                    for the replication of a human.
                    People in this country used to disappear
                    I want to wear pants and be called Jimmie

Translation: I could only guess by the speaker's gestures
what was being spoken to me.
I touched the prism.
He told me it wakes up in light.
He told me it sends a thousand rainbows to the world.

Be kind to that reflection.
This is like a psalm you overheard.
The dark glass fox fraternity.
Bread fist,
pickle island.
Drop the moving snow function.
Misunderstandings, errors, controversy.

We were off by 5 miles

Tricked by sunlines
or many voiced reporting.

January found me.

You make a business of love and give it
to your family of wolves.
I like wolves in the sense of swashbuckling.
Nothing, as the sum of something.
Iva May Rose dies and no one notices.

When he was young he liked his sideburns to come to a point
and tap his ear, anyway no one should be so intimate

Sounds like a bite but has shoulders and looms. Are you fine
if your anger roars up and blows out
your wagging arm. No one
sweeping up after you.

He stops people on the street
for cigarettes

You will never stop
you dream your body will break
if you do

Sugar chest, hunt board,
locked chests for flour,
all things a body might steal

in bags thrown over the back of a horse

[like him, I am longing for 1960]

Things in the hollow got better when money came,
Pa Neal's social security, ten dollars
from Aunt Lillian in California.

Estelle's [scanning, selling books one could barely read]
wild idea: she walks out of the kitchen, grabs
the shovel and from the hill digs a small pine.

                    [I hope we will be wheeled side by side]

Nobody else would take my granddaddy except Estelle
whose mother had been put out on the street in her chair

Ben says, what's so great about clarity?
Sweet chimes made him smile his 13-year-old smile.

When they left me, I was sleeping soundly.
Scratchy Ray chased Holsteins all day.

She cooked breakfast and worked in the cotton field and cooked dinner and worked in the cotton field and cooked supper and out in the garden picked a mess of beans and broke them all before sleeping

This is the map of my body in this house as I remember it

Here: red rocks, red earth so close to dug rock wells.

Psalms,
not palm trees.

The information is the same.

2 dead trees
1 dead tree at pond
Door for manhole
Vitex tree [mega superstar for Texas]
The roadhouse
Quail, forever
The CB bank statement
9 bottles: Melatonin, Vitamin E, Joint Capsules, Carnitine, Gamma Aminobutyric Acid, Sleep essentials, Fish Oil, Sleep aid

The fishmonger told us straight it wasn't the best choice, a bottom dweller.
That damn dog sucking eggs, huff huff

He is teaching me to talk and listening to Tom T Hall
He is teaching me to throw a ball and listening to the Oak Ridge Boys

6 shotguns in the case

The big bottom drawer where they kept the 8 tracks
Elvis, Statler Brothers, Crystal Gayle, and Paul Simon,
who we thought was a country singer

The great silence

A stray dog says GET OUT FROM HERE!

Cicadas rapt with the Nashville sky
only bite if they mistake your arm for a tree branch

They call Butter a little biter

Abe Gingrich sucks salt through his teeth

He would like to be a Mennonite
They talk that German to each other

10 generations ago his people came from Antrim

Now the American Farmer
but there was more to this place than the KKK

Sticky tears, alpha males we talk
about your end

I stand away from the hives until he calls me close
She was going through the change of life and his father-in-law had
      warned him

He will tell you the heart is wicked but decide for yourself dear

At the Hot Eye, iron pool, or lithium,

                      dear Abigail

I only want toast and coffee

                      having already eaten

bless the talkers, bless the shaky waitress

                    My butter   My ocean

My cotton|wood

Her necklace was believable
Her Mary Janes were believable

My Meriwether Lewis rides into the woods that last time, 1809

His honey hives make me salivate;
bluebirds and tiny apartments for purple martins
spiky, spry holly

I'm Methuselah, I just
outlast them

                                        The girl cries when I weed the tall grass

A functional language means everyone moves
The sacs of the body, double-bagged

He makes experiments in collapse and return.
Shoots *Gunsmoke* right out of the television.

The most famous orthopedic surgeon in America holds a sacrum and lumbar spine in his left hand while his right lingers on the coccyx. He's smiling but his lips are stiff.

His whole body covered in white, like a beekeeper, but his face, open to be stung.

I tell you I am watching orchids bloom in my body.

Black pitch in a back drawer.

Sound layered like a flower my hands press.

A man can't open windows in this body.

Must I follow the zipper if I want to be.

Boy in a fox body.
Boy of the marlins.
Snapping turtle boy.
Boy captain,
boy of the crab nebula.
Boy night, boy terror.
Boy sticks and digger,
boy deltoids.

Proportion of boy,
boy slather—
boy in an Easter dress,
boy address, boy orchid.
I never saw him with insects.

I gave him baby aspirin like candy
but shorted him half

On his frayed map, pins where he had whistled boy songs

July would finally laugh, we whispered

a June bug, legs tied with thread

a conspicuous and relatively abrupt change in its body structure

His long leaning out to the world
hyperextend a fifth shoulder
more likely he was spinning his ribs
brachiating around the chicken coop
boy octopod, deep diver legs

[the red ocean will be my classroom]

Always a boy and his dog wandering over the surface of the moon
kick off dust before entering a room

tiny violins inside the violins
but he leaves flares while the dog howls at the earth

I am only this bone standing upright

A man earns a living making sand sculptures
Patients on stone tables made cold with dust
A man comes with an automobile but there is only ice inside
I will need a swat team to touch the body
The hardest part is that the fisherman walks by noticing your camera
Two men work and no need to say anything as they do it
We stay and fill April

I wasn't lost this time but the laughing dog approached
The bones carry invertebrate thoughts like *if I cut the pine down I can see*
   better

You will learn to switch all the pronouns as you open the storeroom

Twirling body shedding
the earth breaks everywhere

By the time he was five he spoke three languages but the teachers thought
   he was retarded
because they couldn't understand

    We built a fire but the wind blew the smoke back in the house

Were it not for the fascia holding me, I'd split

Back palatine plates
like our mother the titmouse

Consider the weight of the double bag or
the bone rings a haversian canal

My cells just got in line and stood up to dance

I know what I might play on the fingerboard but can I run the length of
the swell in time

He beats his chest and laughs,
    it's a tom tom

Let me ask the body
what does it feel like to be full of space

a decade of women in the market with me, flooded with their egg bread

Someone trying to improve me but you know what comes after

Look at how you're dressed, she says and I look

What country is this sewing your cheeks shut

I'm listening to no one slipping in the water

Though my mother spun glass I did not buy it

I walk out with wives in my hands, a woman paid to laugh

The people here are not shy

                                                            Diving birds
            Octopod felt

Wipe off this shining night
or drop the shoulders in fear of flying

            roost roost

you hear music makes him nest
where no one else can sleep

There you were twirling twilight skirts

Stallions in the eyes of cicadas who pump their abdomens fast
just to drown out the 747s landing at the Nashville airport

Jason and the Argonauts in baseball uniforms
Jules just their taxi driver

Means nothing to see

Means glass houses in grass
for her plastic ponies to graze

They've busted my teeth chewing small grain

You will be given a card to link yourself with the hive

Gull above boy with hand raised
          boy sitting at table waving

There is no color, there is a chair with petals

Twin of the great silence

Worker bees rob the bleeding hearts
—they are pink like his ears are pink

          under the tide
they can't tell just who
we favor

Apparatus for Manufacturing Sunset

It meant to our bodies 5 suitcases. I cleaved to this man but carry my own. A start packet. Two of things: dishes, forks, teacups, cloth napkins, spoons (soup and tea), like going away for an eternal picnic. Then singles or multiples: paring knife, cutting board, sugar cubes, vitamins. On the way, across the Atlantic by plane, across Sweden by train, window, hard seats, 56 A and B, the smell of bicycles, fleece, flat green, later recording our voices in the little kitchen speaking for fun with British accents. Hold your mouth shaped like an O and say A for the Swedish sounds. Something slight a little sour. We put our bodies on the floor beside. Below the landlord's a garden with apple trees she offered to us. Two bicycles. We rode toward sea straight into wind. Photographed ourselves cheeks close together standing on 500 million year old bedrock. I learned to make apple cake and gave it away. We walked lightly over moss in birch forests deceptively young.

Every day I walked past single family homes to open field split by path and passed a bench and beside the sea I squatted.

I don't know how to say what kind of foreigners we were.

oo

I never would've come without him but feel the women I knew were what bound me to the place as much as the sea. Song of the closed mouth I don't miss. I was tired of passages but flipped through the magazines you offered. Taxi my body forth, the salt licks of cows I put my arms around necks. In the hidden city, he misses me

I am ever gone

So deeply heard. My little mother goes to beddy-bye. I knew her as a smiling girl who has pushed a baby out, who has cradled fat flesh. Across the street a man paces his apartment, must he make his churning walk

O my beauty at least we are alone

My ears scratched and I didn't want to make sounds I could hear

Every day the sea and every day I didn't hear it
See this glass eye?

A woman caught in the waves, choking as he watched from shore

Peri | cardiac

Breakwater makes a dough and kneads it; flum flum. You think this a train

but we're circulating blood in these tunnels

Skin hunger | skein

Packing a life among stones. Infants coming in wind, skipping the roof

They're waiting in line for bodies

Believe me there are more bodies

I have wanted freedom to watch the crow flight from beginning to end
and not be bothered

The old couple hang clothes together; orange blossom; he teaches her

Yesterday all the summer they'll see. All sizes of body walking into stores taking off clothes (wraps; tankinis; beach cover ups; polo shirts; belted blazers; tarragon turtlenecks)

An old man playing mandolin licks his teeth

By twilight the masses find home, light small peat fires that will puff up the night

The sea near but doesn't interrupt us

I wanted to keep looking through the window at the Amish children but
my little mother drove us away

Just eyes
while the pelvis now scans for little lights

Tracks crossed by green vines   once laughing

Didn't I need to know the destination | test information

Put music on the lip   while behind the sky a cockpit
O the man in my little mother's spine

suspended over the sea like a cable car between two mountains

unused for years

In the dark kitchen the satellite brain to winter burns::
pilot to bombardier   *come in*   *bombardier*

I think of his farm pound pound

the cormorant's song: *Go don't go Go don't go*

            I believe that little red airplane said something to me as it swished by

Slept in my coat three nights
My canary toward   some unmanned myth craft

accumulated hours without meaning (to)
I was what they called a sack of potatoes

                            How would I fight the flying—

:: coral bits, shells with worm holes, shells with wine sheen,
fishing nets hung in large boulders holding back the sea::

This is like reporting in from a meditation

It was a woman who made us think of flying in the first place

Had no way to tell you where I came from   hair brushed stiff

These woods just objects substituted for a broken suitcase
and lack of any reason to photograph the event

I don't want to create my own ancestors in places I know you will find
          interesting

Fancy papered with Victorian family scenes
                                        Boys twisting their hair

          just leave, the tatting

Those girls in train windows busy crocheting the shore

In a crowded sleeping car, the man scuttles into me before I have a chance

Perhaps

I drove the horse when it was still a bridge

Why is a town a place really built to make you a stranger

You hear this butterfly flapping aluminum wings?
It's one person slipping over the Atlantic

there are uneven numbers of people laughing

I make the record of my body shipped to you

[She piles her hair and pins the circles; they snicker]
[people you'll never know]

They make it seem like we're having a conversation
even now
about how we met
I check for small paper messages
ball for birds   nesting with us

Sleep the censure;   wandering fires,
this island ends

and her chain smoking ends
Pilfering ends.

Ash ends, trying to hang onto

the world ends.

Companions,
Corps of Discovery

first is

to discover a shape in the dark

a stone in the palm of your sleep

the waves rolling in dream

even to the one beside your body
spilling drop by drop

no one would believe this but that's precisely what made it noble

the memory of flight

allemansratt (every man's right) falls away

In the limestone desert
in rocks that once were sea

a small drop

landing in the ocean and yet
attended   like coronation

below us, pasted barns and subdivisions
society rewards the settlers

but talk to trees

This must be how the others feel   I was christened

You can go where you are not wanted
think those places slowly

without actually breaking skin

long stories the world upside down   it happens

only told they steal children in fairy tales

                                        reverse and go around the wrong way

not even human beings

                        that's a good one

now I live on the edge of civilization

                                        o salamander eye, travel well

Azulene cloud a little island ocean

next bamboo crackles the heat

A neighbor beats with a stick
some backwards glance to the forest light

ferns curling back up to beginnings

                        was there darkness before my birth?

a quarter of a century, a centaur

                                  time for space
                                  space for time

he had sewn elephant skin
blown the body full of air

or stood stones upright to show the way   toward the future

they follow,   they take off, and children

little worker bees
they bury the dead

with handful
after handful of desert dirt

a shop full of prayers on single yellowed sheets

I don't have time to be angry   brother died young

shin bone just a line to prop a door

entering the room in which I roam

sweet Jesus the roads just pulled us in,

left by the
left by the

We heard they still had grandmothers and we wanted one

I couldn't say whether we'd be back

We wrote home just sitting under night

when I telephoned the convent to ask for information

                                        no name
                                        nor did she receive another
                                        name

by which she might've known *novitiate*

they put me under   I wore white stockings

I wore
my grandmother's legs

Pretend love is a rocket, small salad greens
I note by the seasons

I want to be a beautiful
answerphone

impromptu meetings on limestone hills:

                                        I wasn't lost

Dear___:

I felt so badly about having
to call off tonight's dinner, but unfortunately
my little girl had to be operated on again and
the house is full of doctors and trained
nurses, and on top of it all, my cook has
taken sick so the whole household is in
shambles...

Cordially,
...
NM

Dear___:

I took the picture down to McCall's
yesterday and they were crazy about it, so I guess
you won't have to pose anymore. By lifting the
mouth a little and doing the modeling around it
correctly I believe I'll have a likeness of you...

Cordially,
... N
November 25th

What's the hair but ashes

you believe her speech slower

                                  sing, by which melting snow
                                  felt my heat

she wants
one mint on her tongue at a time

Come upon a woman standing under a dome
singing

                                  this is for Para
                                  you know

No, thereafter

I held quiet as long as I could

A child in the car behind   *O my O my O my*

A woman alone for 54 days
finishing her work

Gypsy. Roving spirit. Has no attachment to the city of Berlin

In the hierarchy of victims, you are either fighter or victim

The enemy can see your light, they said

my country
inside the country

when you meet horses

you keep your hands completely still

A solid chestnut, one white spot

I read signals

                                        Am I close? closed?

I stop early waiting

Even my neck didn't look back

Beside me, the wind swirled
blown sideways

I felt as though I was always there

Never we were not going to meet in this way

Someone watches but doesn't photograph

A train just a line crossing or merging

how does it know in snow

And when the earth turns I'm facing west

some yarrow, only useful

That evening I was quiet

I believed a song was boarding

Roam

Light gets through beside the column; pigtails

she's crossed her ankles, sits in the long diagonal of steps, sun;

behind her a woman with a wind of dress, those folds; of the girl's shrug,
what's Italy anyhow but a place where folks live with repeating stone
arches?

A woman wearing wind coming toward her; this action repeats
the bricks stack up. You down a road somewhere, arches
in your feet too pressing and retracting.

That girl wore sandals which gave her a blister on her right heel before she
can pronounce Achilles, ribbons limping around pigtails, gingham print
dress a high waist, hair braided with skill along her crown.

Two columns of braid, column behind her carved up

as icing on a birthday cake she saw once in a window
down a quiet street in a city

she can now only remember without colors.

I tried telling him the music was too loud once, boy was that a bad idea. It didn't occur to him to change the whole structure of the telephone system inviting all that feedback, but just the play of it was enough to set him to combing his hair through, a madman. Before that, it was all magic p's walking along the rivers he loved, shooting into space and back again. He was tuned to those who won't step on cracks. Couldn't bear any significant numbers in his life that weren't somehow prime. As I said, it didn't occur to me, so maybe we can play it back again, those echoes he talked about, someone must have taken it down.

How did I get in the brown tug? Fantastic commitment to your sternum full of softness. My teeth chattering too long when M. wanted to swim to the middle and lie on granite's side. Never seen pictures of whales doing what I said I was afraid of. Where could I go anyhow it was only the nerves talking. I saw you once measuring my tapping foot. We swam evening. A boat capsized you inside. Would longing be there after I was on my backstroke to arrive? Please know I'm never weeding. Thorny body. She told me she hates hers boy is it hard to look at. I offered to walk her home but you know I'm not Nebraska. When it comes to calibrating shyness, I'm shy. A rattling go at jealousy, the kind I wish swept floors. Thin dust settles on the green-segmented caterpillar. Some verticals are horizons. So then, your body walking on water. If I see you in the window I've departed. My love's gone sleeping without which we touch. Repeat: send the watch and chain he keeps time with.

When they entered, a child stood in the door, waiting to cross the threshold, looking back into other waiting rooms, then smiling. I couldn't wake any earlier. The dreams blew up in my face; each day made mention of his birdcall, the rock crows. Sky passing over and we see only chaos going past. I had his chair, was devoted, his sounds I recreated from nothing but books. I made my throat folds into choreography and banged it out, first with piano *piano piano* but too late and too loud, come the chair, come vagrants, come throat folds on the horizon. I was the instance: why go up in the tower when everything around is inflamed? You see my measure you lay it down you make it deep in the pot and the roots, you take the spade and speak while waving your hands, and if they listen, if they listen, come morning together the baking will be easy will be what you lost. Then the plants die away and come back just like I already said to you; my map here will keep the scent of you.

After they got news of new cells, a baby's cry. Music hovering on the sill. A pattering: we spoke on the phone into wooden boxes, broken toaster, chopsticks. The wind swelled like squall. Was that the sound to put in a pocket? She said, God loved the donkeys and blessed them. She said, we ate cake, being husband, being wife; our words gave flight such as beauty rises, early in the morning, otherwise we have no chance. There's loyalty then also the small dove we feed come window, chasing its kind, leaving nests half-built, combing rats from our hair.

Narcissus the only one moving in that room. Four rooms, and the hero walking over them all day. A huge slab of century. All archipelago with no bridges. The hero in old age, tossing coins in dry fountains, which are diverted, covered in plastic, yet still charging tourists to enter. Toes and their tissues keeping everyone away from sinister heels that don't hit the ground. What rot. The city passes me. Cobblestones keyed in place, a poverty of old age, more ornate than either of us expected at the time, we used to say. Who laid all this marble near the glass? I slept on the floor from sickness. It was like lying on the dead body of Death.

From our position, there is no future, there is only our position wearing us like clothes over our bones, or vice versa, but there is still no future, yet. Inside this position, we don't need to plan for what is next because we are soft. I am not yet going up the stairs, I am perched beside the bottom stair, and from this position I can see the person sitting at their kitchen table across the courtyard, reading a newspaper. This informs me as well. I can also see that sometimes it is not easy to be inside the self or its dimensions. And this would be my error, in this state, looking inside to the other, rather than looking inside my own. Because being inside myself I can feel my own being too, I can feel myself at the bottom stair, the person across the courtyard reading, maybe something in their manner speaks to me, and from my own position I consider what is being said.

The body in the out of place world. Knocking. I've got jaws. Plain laws. Fortifications. I can show this to you, this entire world, by the time we're 94. I'm never telling another soul how old I am. The spider plants and their jets and inflatable roots coming for me across the room. The story was boring; anyone could tell it. Up and down the stairs five times a day, holy holy holy. Someone in the building lost a set of keys and leaves a note on the front door. Someone in the building finds a set of keys and leaves a note on the second floor window of the side house, and a set of numbers with at least two missing. Letter after letter comes in the mail for the person who used to live here. The ground moving under us, into the house at four. He came home and found me here, hat pulled over my eyes and laid beside me and entered dreams of his own, began speaking out of them to me across a window ledge, asked me to go in with him on some land in T____, where neither of us had lived for years.

Transmigration

Trees made of maps with distended stomachs

I leave a mannequin in my place; must I be the only one

busy explorers, not knowing where they go but knowing they go—

I bring switchgrass

and call the doctor with your please button

                                If children sat on the floor

it was 1952 and mothers given away for free

                                Someone used a pillow to prop her

We paid to see one room, it was 1954

                                Eyes made from magazine letters

returned from England

In it, a mechanical man extending a hand

                                I couldn't go back, apparently

                she reused foreign stamps

When I shake your hand

                meaning I do, the body = x,

moves when I move

        The confirmation you must write to me

§

I knot it low under my chin

        Sweden will someday be the only place left standing

A road beside shore beside pier

        beside tugs beside unpardonable sand

pinned under unpardonable sea,

        out the tug goes, out brine

My little mother loved the smell of my body

        or perhaps days she wished me in the dumpster

a life made mostly of sticky lollipops

        A man takes a woman, and they take the train

Four times transfer, where they take the train

        No one gets on but they ride, day follows itself

§

I can leave my prayers anywhere I choose. I let my piss fly

Those who oscillate side to side or
those who stand in place

                                      My god, it smelled like doves
                                      as he walked past

No one kicking a name over my stilts

I slip on a faded dress
Isn't it enough

I threw her in the air when she was small

This just the place I start and a place I come back to

§

Touching your body like opening returned letters

If there are ghosts   let them be photographed in profile

The outside epidermis loose
so I must feel around for the Boca Raton memories

Curtains spliced from 1964

There are such things as failed transplants

§

I don't want to start with the body in a bottle

It has a red label   it is a peninsula
                                        sectioned pricking

Measure the sore back by | tears from the eye sides

touch his chest it's 1967

When asleep | heart in sack
double dribble | flowering legs

Half the reason I came by

                    his father

                                            his sister no longer
                                  ballet lessons

how his feet long stuck in tiptoe

§

We might forthcoming droughts withhold love

but here the bees come close to saying :: a labor of small flapping wings

We sleep in the Pigeonnier where once rabbits slept
                                    glass faces underneath glass fur

This house older than America

A box for butterflies & inlaid lid with bone and a sectioned spine, like mine

§

I will die somewhere like this,
surrounded by humans who I hope will also die

he said, unflinching

        Didn't we wake laughing to a bully crow?

I must weed the windows loose

in their faces, after time, what ailed
curved them to distress

Where he listened there was some serial   unfolding

§

I stood on the ridge swallowing down my armor

                            the chicanery of passport check

                            men selling fruit in shade
                            tracing lay lines

Bivouac | caravan
I keep separate my love

We carry our belongings around like tinkers

              That's two Swedish miles
              of skin, straight shins

Isn't the moon late tonight?

One locus on the new cobblestone
our street of which I am always planting

                       (sweet Jesus of Nazareth)

walks for free through open fields

§

I won't do much more than touch the back of your skull with my fingertips

He sees the peacock butterfly because he waits

I don't dream of my father's sister   that worries me

my life will come
and go like this

where in one place distant from me

I want to always smell sea in my hair

§

this, this;

before

a woman named Eden trapped in the wall of a house
whose mascot is a porcelain teapot

The superhero falling backwards with a child

[I don't dream of his father either]

Of course I am in this room—
the atmosphere pressure killing me but I hover close in the paling
covers. I graze

A woman kisses me. A mother kisses me, wearing wool

Two sisters hold hands in a distant house
The sun balloons behind them

The ghost came and left
My songs are sociable if you listen

I wash the wash it down I
go

This the
beginning

§

We curtailed; I rifled through drawers in that house

                                        paper parasols for tiny dolls,
                                        paraffin molds, matchbooks
                                        marked *external use only*
                                        followed by *please* and
                                        wooden skewers

they last and last

I'm busy watching my dead grandfather drive
the yellow school bus I've taken a seat in

You want to get away?

The perfect atlas, your broken spine

I can't make my failings missed trains flying on Persian rugs

I met you at the cemetery

You'd get back there eventually

§

see children
the sun goes down

not the heart itself

sack governing   joy or sadness

I never dream of   I never dream of

sweet flower   red gum tree
                                  horse hair

tweet tweet when I appeared aloof

A stand of peony stalks
                                  I sang I sang I sang; aspen bank hung on

The white gospel of losing the body altogether

        Some glad morning
        I will feel the ground underneath me

            This is my work of tiny starflowers   new winged flies

            The bee's dance tells them   next home

                        drag the lake
                    there's still no body

One-Way Street

...the secret blemish on the loved body, where they duck down,
safe and sound. And no passer-by will guess that it is here,
precisely here, in the shortcoming... that the admirer's burst
of love, swift as an arrow, hits home...
—Walter Benjamin

I buried the ghost children
gone a hunting—

though they squirmed I combed their hair and changed the mattress

I spoke in a dark room

the words came back

which is not what I mean to say I was on the train

An elder

Surrounded by bright buildings, windows

I was transcribing your letters

was haunting

§

Some lines still existed though not used by public

You said, I fear the document of my own life no one will find

One had fire
Another earth

Peopled
populus

My swearing in

I don't remember how you pinned her to the world; I never remember

§

A hidden city

hidden in tunnels

its people trying to move under ground, in trains
by shovel or hand

Someone heard there was there a line from here to Dresden

All the traces of people waiting throughout time

footprints mark the way ::
:: they are erasable

what is left
what is left
what is left

they go

§

To feel only full of phrases

but the body speaks fluidly without stops

They tried to tell you the future a one-way street

We came and set them right

Mismatch :: mislead

without fail your whirl of letters

Stock pot calling but mother doesn't answer
The child the hunter of things

My mind at last goes round the city park

§

Your accordion, swollen with heartbreak
A plain bird sharpening its beak on a twig

The sun slung its arm like a lover finding a shoulder—what you called autumn. At windows, over streets, two walked past in a line, space before and after them also a line, their bodies' bulk

You thought any civilization could recover a sense of the miraculous

An outline of children standing in a window,
drawn in white

      they pronounce silently
      without murmuring
      having lost the habit of talking over others

That shine or stretching of time as if you too forgot to breathe.

If I had my way, I'd record them speaking their names and their mother's name into a microphone attached to a map so that when they left

auratic perception

It wouldn't take them long to spot the titmouse—

§

The whole notion of one-way street
means some things you can no longer face

Within hours 50 to 100 persons a day

In cars added to the rear of passenger trains

running on time

Underground tunnels – escapades, or worse—

ja, ja, we who do or do not do

The yo-yo, face down I planted

                              they were child seeds

so long have you been waiting here
            the flute curled up in my ears

of the wish to sleep
instead of breathing into melamine dinnerware

A small boy walks along tracks

                        I cannot swing myself side to side
                        waiting on kindness

§

May tuberculosis take you

May the leaves cover your body
and make respectable

a holy day for which we made lists

A means of overlap: standing by the screen door
the bullets won't enter
your ghost body

I believe you can remake the structures
around yourself by reversing
the motion you are about to make

I believe in the trace of your fingers along
the handrail, and in the button
that opens doors on car number seven.

If I don't touch the people
If I touch objects those people have touched

My body forms to the warm seat facing backwards
you have just vacated

My illness speaks
                with a twang

§

That house is *fire*
I'm going *fahr*

I never thought of cities as places people actually lived

Here small subtleties: that's the piano
making racket, you say
and purr

The difference could not be photographed

A woman claimed she filmed ghost children playing
in her basement

        Tunnels dug under buildings on Bernauer Straße,
        enter number __ and come out in number __

The dialect gives them away, they
stop minding

This is not your train; this is not your name

§

I heard a child's voice calling *me me me me*
under the window

I gave them money and they promised
At first it was easy. I colored my hair

I did what they told me. Make your teeth flat
when you speak. I read the papers but my tongue

is like a buttoned flap

I don't know what happens in my mouth when I smile

This the middle of love

§

There is a line and a current moving up the line making sparks

It was as if I had landed somewhere without having had a view to begin with

        You stood in the door like she said I didn't
        see you

I hoped someday to have as much presence as a stone

how else would I think about children
hauling coffins

arms extended

Acknowledgements

Apparatus for Manufacturing Sunset appeared in a chapbook from dancing girl press by the same title.

One-Way Street appeared in *VERSE*. (Fall 2015)

A piece of information about his invisibility and *Companions, Corps of Discovery* appeared as chapbooks from MIEL Books. (2012)

Excerpts from *Transmigration* appeared online at *Ostrich Review*.

Letters from Neysa McMein to Amelia Earhart reprinted with permission from the Neysa McMein estate. Thanks to Elizabeth Wilkinson at Purdue University. These letters found at MSP 9, The George Palmer Putnam collection of Amelia Earhart papers, Karnes Research Center, Purdue University Libraries.

Thanks

Roam marks a migration, back, forth and round again. Thanks to so many people and places who supported this work by offering temporary landings: Praia de Luz, Kalmar, Mirandol, Abiquiu, Campbellsville, Husartorpet, and Os Figueiros. APOI was written in residence in Beeston UK, at Eireann Lorsung's house. CCOD was written in residence in The Burren, Ireland. *Roam* and *One-Way Street* owe a great debt to Berlin.

Thanks to: Éireann Lorsung for her continuous and generous support of my work, and for carrying on; Dave Wasserman for the enormous creative space he has made at Os Figueiros; Sylvia and Henrik for their bit of big Swedish sky; and A. Ravi for coming along.

A Piece of Information About His Invisibility is for my brother, David.